MOJANG STUDIOS

MINECRAFT

ENGLISH
OFFICIAL WORKBOOK
AGES 7-8

P

F

B

T

JON GOULDING
AND DAN WHITEHEAD

INTRODUCTION

HOW TO USE THIS BOOK

Welcome to an exciting educational experience! Your child will go on a series of adventures through the amazing world of Minecraft, improving their written English skills along the way. Matched to the National Curriculum for writing for ages 7–8 (Year 3), this workbook takes your child into fascinating landscapes where our heroes Kim and Sami embark on building projects and daring treasure hunts…all while keeping those pesky mobs at bay!

As each adventure unfolds, your child will complete topic-based questions worth a certain number of emeralds . These can then be 'traded in' on the final page. The more challenging questions are marked with this icon  to stretch your child's learning. Answers are included at the back of the book.

MEET OUR HEROES

Kim is one of the best warriors in the world – or at least that is what she likes to tell people! She always wants to craft the best weapons and armour and will explore far and wide to find rare materials. Although Kim is not yet the legendary fighter she claims to be, she is loyal and brave and will defend her friends from mobs, no matter how deadly!

Sami just loves to wander. He is incredibly curious and is always the first to dig into an interesting looking cave, or dash into a new biome to see what he can find. He sometimes forgets to think a situation through before carrying out his actions, but he can always rely on help from his friend Kim!

First published in 2021 by Collins
An imprint of HarperCollins*Publishers*
1 London Bridge Street, London, SE1 9GF

HarperCollins*Publishers*
Macken House, 39/40 Mayor Street Upper,
Dublin 1, D01 C9W8, Ireland

Publisher: Fiona McGlade
Authors: Jon Goulding and Dan Whitehead
Project management: Richard Toms
Design: Ian Wrigley and Sarah Duxbury
Typesetting: Nicola Lancashire at Rose and Thorn Creative Services
Minecraft skins courtesy of Claudia 'ZestyKale' Faye
Special thanks to Alex Wiltshire, Sherin Kwan and Marie-Louise Bengtsson at Mojang and the team at Farshore
Production: Karen Nulty

MOJANG STUDIOS

ISBN 978-0-00-846282-6

British Library Cataloguing in Publication Data.

A CIP record of this book is available from the British Library.

10 9 8 7 6 5 4 3

Printed in India by Multivista Global Pvt. Ltd.

FSC
MIX
Paper | Supporting responsible forestry
FSC™ C007454
www.fsc.org

This book contains FSC™ certified paper and other controlled sources to ensure responsible forest management.

For more information visit: www.harpercollins.co.uk/green

CONTENTS

TRANSCRIPTION AND SPELLING

FAR FROM PLAIN!

Don't make the mistake of thinking the plains are boring. Just because so many Minecraft adventures start there, and just because they don't have the exciting novelty features of more exotic biomes, doesn't mean that the plains are unable to offer lots of menacing mobs and lovely loot. You just have to get out there and find it!

SWORD SEARCH

The day has started with Kim frantically searching the chests in the house she has built with Sami. Her diamond sword has gone missing!

PREFIXES 1

Prefixes are groups of letters added to the beginning of words. They change the meaning of the original word. The prefixes *un-*, *dis-* and *mis-* all have negative meanings. For example, *lucky* becomes <u>un</u>lucky, *agree* becomes <u>dis</u>agree and *hear* becomes <u>mis</u>hear.

Kim is cross that she cannot find her sword. She and Sami have planned to go on a big adventure today, but without her best weapon Kim is worried she will miss it.

1

Underline the prefix in each word in the boxes in the first row. Then draw lines to the sentence in which each word would fit best.

disappear	misplaced	unlucky

Kim was _____ to lose her diamond sword.	It seemed to just _____ !	Kim had _____ her sword.

2

Insert the correct prefix (*un-*, *dis-* or *mis-*) into the words below.

a) _____ usual

b) _____ kind

c) _____ trust

d) _____ tidy

e) _____ able

f) _____ obey

COLOUR IN HOW MANY EMERALDS YOU EARNED

PREFIXES 2

Some prefixes are used to make nouns that have different meanings to the original noun or adjective. For example, the prefix *sub-* means *under* and it can be added to the word *marine* (which refers to the sea) to make the word *submarine*.

Kim and Sami search everywhere. The sword is nowhere to be found.

1

Read the sentences. Write the prefix from each highlighted word.

a) Kim wished her sword would just reappear. ....

b) She would have to return to their dig for
more diamond ore. ....

c) She wished there was a supermarket that
sold swords! ....

2

Choose the best word from the box to fit into each sentence.

interact	submerged	autobiography	international

a) If Kim wrote a book about her life, it would be an

....

b) To open a chest, Kim must .... with it.

c) If she had dropped her sword in the lake, it would be

....

Kim does not want to set off on a new adventure without her best weapon. There is only one thing to do!

3

Read the text below. Find the four examples of words with prefixes and use them to complete the table.

Kim's sword is not going to reappear and she knows she will have to return to the place where she found the diamond ore and mine some more ore. There will be no time to interact with the villagers on the way. After having a rest and some food to refresh herself, she prepares to set off.

Word	Prefix	Root word

4

Find out and explain the meaning of the prefixes below.

a) re- ....

b) anti- ....

c) inter- ....

d) auto- ....

SUFFIXES

A suffix is a letter or group of letters added to the end of a word to change the meaning. If a suffix begins with a vowel (*-ing, -er, -ed,* or *-en,* for example) and the original (root) word has more than one syllable and ends with a consonant, the consonant is often doubled (for example: *forgot – forgotten*). Some suffixes such as *-ation* change the word class (for example, the verb *inform* becomes the noun *information*).

Kim tells Sami she will be back soon and heads out into the plains to find the place she had previously mined diamond ore. If only she could remember where it was.

 1

Underline the suffix in each of the highlighted words in the text below.

Kim was starting to get tired. She would have expected to find the mine by

now but, because she had forgotten, her frustration was growing.

2

Write the root word that each of these words are created from.

a) beginning ....

b) preferred ....

c) information ....

d) forgetting ....

As Kim searches, she is startled by a group of creepers. Luckily she still has her bow. Get ready for a battle, Kim!

 3

Add the suffix *-ation* to each verb in the box. Use the noun it forms in the appropriate sentence.

tempt	consider	relax	confront

a) The battle began! There would be no .... on this trip after all.

b) It was an action-packed .... with the creepers.

c) She had to resist the .... to use her tipped arrows.

d) With the creepers defeated, she had to give serious .... to where she was going to go next.

 4

 Look at the pairs of words in the boxes. Each verb has been changed to a noun with the addition of the suffix *-ation*. Explain what you notice about the change to these words when the suffix is added.

prepare – preparation	adore – adoration	sense – sensation

....

....

....

THE SUFFIX -LY

The suffix -ly is added to an adjective to form an adverb. For example, sad becomes sadly. Care is needed with root words of more than one syllable ending in y with a consonant before it (for example, merry). In these cases, the y is replaced by i before adding -ly (for example, merrily).

Kim knows she is in the right area now, but still can't see the hole she had dug last time she found the diamond ore. Where is it?

1

Add the suffix -ly to each of the words below.

a) sad.............

b) complete.............

c) final.............

d) actual.............

e) honest.............

f) quick.............

g) exact.............

h) fair.............

2

Words ending in -le have the -le removed before adding -ly. Change the highlighted word in each example below.

a) Kim was sensible looking for the hole.

She looked for the hole ....

b) She found it simple to locate the entrance.

She .... located the entrance.

c) The approach to the hole was a fiddle.

The approach to the hole was ....

Kim is so busy hurrying to the hole she had dug before that she does not notice one more sneaky creeper. It's too late...BOOM!

3

In the text below, find the adjectives which need changing to adverbs with the addition of -ly. Write the adverbs in the spaces provided.

Kim was injured and moved feeble. If she hadn't been wearing armour, she would possible have been killed. She angry threw her bow down and sad sat on the floor next to it. She soon cheered up. Happy, she had lots of food and was going to be complete okay.

....

....

....

4

♥ Look at the pairs of words in the boxes. Each adjective has been changed to an adverb which ends in -ly. Write the 'rule' for adding the suffix to these words.

| basic – basically | dramatic – dramatically | frantic – frantically |

....

....

....

THE SUFFIX -OUS

Adding the suffix *-ous* can turn a noun into an adjective. Sometimes *-ous* appears when there is no root word or obvious root word. For words ending in *our*, the *u* is removed before adding *-ous* (for example, *vigour* becomes *vigorous*).

After restoring her health and checking for any more sneaky creepers, Kim ventures back into the tunnels she had dug last time.

1

Insert the suffix *-ous* to the words in these sentences.

a) She thought this adventure was danger............... .

b) Kim knew spiders could be venom............... .

c) With no food left, if she got bitten it would be very seri............... .

2

Find all the examples of *-ous* endings in the text below. Write the words in the spaces provided.

The enormous tunnel stretched out in front of her. Kim was curious to explore more. She knew that there were various dangers but it could be a tremendous adventure.

....

....

Kim reaches the spot where she had found diamond ore last time and begins digging to see if there is any more. She has to balance high above the lava to get there.

3

Give each highlighted word an *-ous* ending. Make any other changes to the word as necessary.

a) It would not be very humour if Kim fell into the lava.

....

b) Doing all this digging was not very glamour. ....

c) She had a rigour afternoon of mining ahead. ....

4

For each pair of words below, explain what has happened to allow *-ous* to be added.

a) vary   various

....

b) courage   courageous

....

c) fame   famous

....

SAME SOUND, DIFFERENT SPELLING

The long *a* sound is often spelled *a_e* as in *same*, or *ai* as in *train*. There are other spellings though – *ei*, *ey* and *eigh*. Similarly, the short *u* sound as in *cup* is sometimes spelled *ou*.

Kim breaks through into a large, underground cave. She can see the unmistakable glitter of diamond ore on the other side but there are also lots of zombies moaning in the gloom.

1

Shade in the five boxes which have words that contain a long *a* sound.

late	plains	zombie	answer
villager	daisy	prey	eight

2

Find the four examples of words in the text below with the short *u* spelled *ou*. Write the words in the spaces provided.

Kim saw two, then four zombies! Double the amount! This meant she was in trouble. With no food left to heal with, just one touch from a zombie could be a disaster.

....

....

Kim doesn't have enough arrows to fight all the zombies. She must stay out of their reach as she runs across the cave to the diamond ore!

3

For each given word, make up a sentence about exploring a cave full of zombies.

a) wait ....

b) weight ....

c) they ....

d) brave ....

4

Find three examples of words containing each sound to write in the columns of the table.

Long *a* using *ei*	Long *a* using *ey*	Long *a* using *eigh*	Short *u* using *ou*

EXCEPTION WORDS

Some words are tricky to spell because they use different patterns of letters than might be expected from the way they sound. They are exceptions to familiar spelling rules and the words just have to be learned. Some spelling patterns can make several different sounds.

Kim dashes around the edge of the cave. The zombies spot her and move towards her. How can she stay safe while digging out the diamond ore?

1

Complete each sentence with a word from the box which rhymes with the bracketed word for each sentence.

through	thought	enough	although

a) Kim decided that she'd had ....

(huff)

b) She also decided to see this ....

(blue)

c) .... it was tricky, she would do her best.

(low)

d) Suddenly, she had a ....

(sort)

2

Draw lines to join the three words below which rhyme with each other.

purpose	suppose	various	address	promise	famous

Kim has lots of dirt blocks in her inventory. If she moves fast, she can build a wall around herself to keep the zombies away while she digs out the diamond ore.

3

The *ear* spelling pattern is found in several words in the text below. Find these words and write them in the spaces provided. Listen to the sound made by *ear* in each.

Kim was in fear because she could hear the zombies. Her heart was beating fast. Then she heard them again, closer, an early warning of their approach. They stopped when they reached her wall of earth, unable to get through.

....

....

4

Make up a sentence about Kim's adventures for each of the given words in which the *u* is part of a different sound for each.

a)   fruit   ....

b)   guide   ....

c)   busy   ....

CONTRACTED WORDS

When two words such as *do not* are pushed together to make a shorter (or contracted) word – *don't* – an apostrophe is used in place of the missing letter (or letters). Care must be taken to make sure the apostrophe is in the correct place.

Kim quickly mines plenty of diamonds and then puts down her crafting table. She is going to craft a new diamond sword. Those zombies are in trouble now!

1

Draw lines to match each word pair with its contracted form.

should not	don't	she's	they've	you'll

they have	you will	you are

you're	shouldn't	do not	she is

2

Change each pair of underlined words in the passage below to their contracted form.

Kim knew she <u>should not</u> have lost her sword. It <u>could have</u> been worse but <u>she will</u>

never make that mistake again. Even with a diamond sword, it <u>was not</u> easy fighting

this many zombies.

Kim leaves the cave and makes her way back out of her old tunnel. It is already night-time when she emerges. Time to find shelter!

3

Complete the passage with the contracted version of the words in the box.

I will	she would	would not	were not	had not

There .... any trees and she needed wood for shelter.

It .... be so bad but she .... eaten

for a long time either. Kim was sure .... find food and

shelter soon.

" .... keep looking until I find enough wood," she thought.

4

Correct each of the contracted words below and write the full version too.

a) havn't ....

b) wo'nt ....

c) sh'ed ....

d) are'nt ....

COLOUR IN HOW MANY
EMERALDS YOU EARNED

DICTIONARIES

A dictionary contains words in alphabetical order. It can be used to check the spelling and meaning (definition) of words. If the first letter of a word is known, it is easier to find the word in a dictionary. Knowing the second letter helps too because once words have been sorted by the alphabetical order of first letters, they are then ordered by their second letters.

While looking for trees, Kim spots a village close by. She can rest there overnight and head back to see Sami in the morning.

 1

Write some of the things Kim has seen in the plains in alphabetical order. Look at the first letter of each word.

zombie	creeper	sword	village	hole

....

....

2

Kim has seen several things in the plains beginning with the letter *c*.

a) Use the second letter of each word to put them in alphabetical order.

cow	creeper	chicken

....

b) She also saw a cornflower. Explain why this would come before *cow* in alphabetical order.

....

The next day, Kim wakes up refreshed. It is a lovely village and she decides to look around before going home.

3

Kim can imagine that the village has not changed for over a century. Use a dictionary to find the word class and the meaning of the word *century*.

Century is a ....

It means ....

4

The village is very busy. Kim spots a master leatherworker. Their business is selling saddles to ride horses, so she buys one with some emeralds.

a) What do the words *busy* and *business* mean?

The word *busy* means ....

The word *business* means ....

b) Explain the order in which the two words would appear in a dictionary.

....

....

COLOUR IN HOW MANY EMERALDS YOU EARNED

HOMOPHONES

Homophones are words that sound the same but have a different spelling and meaning. It is important to know which homophone to use (and how to spell it) to avoid confusion.

Kim is able to ride a horse all the way home.

1

Circle the correct homophone in each pair of this passage. Use a dictionary to help.

Reign / Rain *started to fall and Kim could* **here / hear** *it splashing on the*

plain / plane. *It soon soaked* **threw / through** *her clothes. This was horrible*

whether / weather *but she was* **not / knot** *bothered — she had a new diamond*

sword. Home was now in sight. Nearly **their / there**, *Kim!*

2

Underline the spelling errors in the sentences below and write the correct spellings (the correct homophones) in the spaces provided.

Kim caught a chicken and eight the meet. She had a large peace. She was very hungry and it tasted grate.

....

....

COLOUR IN HOW MANY EMERALDS YOU EARNED

ADVENTURE ROUND-UP

SAMI'S MESSAGE

When Kim gets back to the house, Sami is nowhere to be seen. He has left a note. He has set out already and tells her to meet him in the bamboo jungle to the east of their home.

NEXT STOP, THE JUNGLE!

Kim is already excited about another adventure. After stuffing her inventory with food from their storage chests, she grabs her diamond sword and heads out to catch up with Sami.

VOCABULARY, GRAMMAR AND PUNCTUATION

JUNGLE ADVENTURE

Kim and Sami are lucky to have spawned near a bamboo jungle. These biomes are quite rare and are home to lots of plants and animals that do not appear anywhere else. From pandas and parrots, to cocoa and melons, it is always worth venturing into these lush biomes whenever they appear.

ITCHING TO GO!

Sami waits and waits for Kim to return from the diamond mine, but she is taking ages! He is itching to start a new adventure and he knows that Kim is an experienced explorer who would be able to survive whatever trouble she might find.

OFF HE GOES!

Sami can't wait any longer! Leaving a note, he treks to the jungle to see what he can find...

CONJUNCTIONS 1

Joining words such as *when, if, that* and *because* are used to link words, phrases and clauses in sentences. They are conjunctions. When two parts of a sentence have equal importance, *or, and,* or *but* are used. For example: *Kim could fight the creeper <u>or</u> she could run away.*

If a joining word is introducing a part of a sentence which does not fully make sense on its own, *when, if, that, although* or *because* are used. For example: *Sami defeated the zombie <u>that had attacked him</u>.*

It is warm and damp in the jungle. As Sami carefully makes his way through the tangle of trees, he thinks about what to do next.

1

Select the best joining word from each pair for each sentence.

a) Sami wants to build a shelter .... **because / although**
    food is needed first.

b) He wants a parrot .... **or / because**
    it would warn him of danger.

c) There are slimes in the way .... **but / when**
    he is not too worried.

2

Complete the sentences using a different conjunction from the box in each one.

> **if   or**

a) Sami could run away ....

b) He knows he will get food ....

CONJUNCTIONS 2

Conjunctions are often used to show cause. For example: *Kim was happy* <u>*because*</u> *she defeated the creeper.* The word *because* introduces what caused her to be happy. Conjunctions can also show when an event happens relative to another event. For example: *They found food* <u>*before*</u> *they built a shelter.* The shelter was built after finding food.

The slobbery slurping sound of the slimes makes Sami feel sick. It is slowly getting dark and he will have to be prepared to fight.

 1

Underline the conjunction in each sentence.

a)   Sami prepares his sword because he will have to fight the slimes.

b)   He uses a potion while he is fighting.

c)   The slimes drop slimeballs when he defeats them.

2

Choose the best conjunction in each pair to write into each sentence.

a)   It is difficult to find the way .... **although / because**
it is starting to get dark.

b)   Sami looks for food .... **when / if**
the slimes are beaten.

c)   Sami came up with a plan .... **or / as**
he explored.

Night will soon fall and Sami knows dangerous mobs will be prowling in even greater numbers.

3

Place a tick in the correct column to show whether the underlined conjunction in each sentence shows *cause* or *time*.

Sentence	Cause	Time
Sami keeps listening for danger <u>while</u> he walks.		
<u>As</u> he is so hungry, he has to find food.		
Sami knows there is trouble <u>when</u> he hears some zombies.		
He runs away <u>because</u> he has no desire for a fight.		

4

Complete each sentence with a suitable conjunction.

a) (cause) Sami needed a tame parrot .... it would warn him of danger.

b) (time) Kim had to go and find diamond ore .... her sword went missing.

c) (time) Sami searched for food .... it got darker.

d) (time) .... it went dark, there was even more danger.

COLOUR IN HOW MANY EMERALDS YOU EARNED

PREPOSITIONS AND ADVERBS

Adverbs of time and place tell the reader when or where something happened or is happening. For example: *Kim decided she would find shelter <u>later</u>. Sami went <u>inside</u>.*

Prepositions describe place and time. For example: *Sami likes adventures <u>in</u> the winter.* (The word *in* gives more detail about when Sami likes adventures.) *They ate their food <u>next to</u> the tree.* (*next to* adds further detail about where they ate.)

Sami quickly builds a small shelter as night falls and places the bed from his inventory inside. He will be safe from the mobs in there.

Underline the preposition in each of these sentences.

a)   The zombie is behind the tree.

b)   Sami sleeps in his shelter.

c)   Sami built his shelter on a hill.

d)   He once slept under the tall trees.

Circle the adverb in each of these sentences.

a)   Sami knows he will need to move on soon.

b)   He might hear zombies later.

c)   Sami does not want to go outside.

d)   He senses danger nearby.

In the morning, Sami continues to explore. From the corner of his eye, he sees a flash of red. A parrot! He follows it through the jungle.

3

Insert a suitable preposition in each sentence.

a) Sami needed to jump .... a stream.

b) He climbed .... the large rock.

c) He had to catch the parrot .... nightfall.

d) The parrot flew .... the trees.

4

For each adverb, write a sentence that explains when or where something happened or will happen in the jungle.

a) soon

....

b) later

....

c) everywhere

....

d) nearby

....

NOUNS AND PRONOUNS

When nouns are repeated too often in a piece of writing, it becomes less interesting to read. Personal pronouns such as *he, she, it* and *they* are used in place of nouns to avoid this repetition.

Sami struggles to keep up with the parrot but he will not let it get away. He really wants a tame parrot!

1

Circle the pronoun in the second sentence of each of these.

a)   Sami chases the parrot. It is fast.

b)   Sami runs to catch up. He is getting closer.

c)   There are lots of trees in the way. They are tall.

d)   Sami finds a melon. It contains seeds that the parrot would like.

2

In each pair of sentences below, the highlighted noun is repeated. Replace the second use of the noun with an appropriate pronoun. Write it in the box.

a)   **The parrot** lands nearby. **The parrot** is red.

b)   **Sami** begins to approach the parrot. **Sami** is going to try to tame it.

c)   **The leaves** are dark green. **The leaves** block the light.

Sami offers the parrot some melon seeds. It gobbles them up greedily. It is now tame! Sami is thrilled to have a pet parrot.

3

Insert suitable pronouns in the spaces in the passage below.

Walking through the trees is an ocelot. Sami wonders if ....

could gain the trust of .... *as well. Creepers would keep away*

because .... *don't like ocelots. The tamed parrot will be useful*

as .... *can warn Sami of hostile mobs too.*

4

 Possessive pronouns can also be used to avoid repeating the same words. Add the correct possessive pronoun to each sentence below.

Example: *Sami built a shelter. The shelter was* <u>his</u>.

a)   Kim has given Sami a sword which is now ....

b)   Together they built a house in the plains. The house is ....

COLOUR IN HOW MANY EMERALDS YOU EARNED

TENSE

The present tense is used when writing about now. For example: *It is morning.* The present tense changes slightly when something is ongoing at the current time. For example: *I am eating my breakfast.*

The past tense is used when writing about something that has happened. For example: *It was morning.* When writing about an ongoing action in the past, it changes slightly. For example: *I was eating my breakfast.*

Sami's tame parrot sits on his shoulder. What a cool pet! Suddenly it starts copying the hiss of a creeper. That means some are nearby.

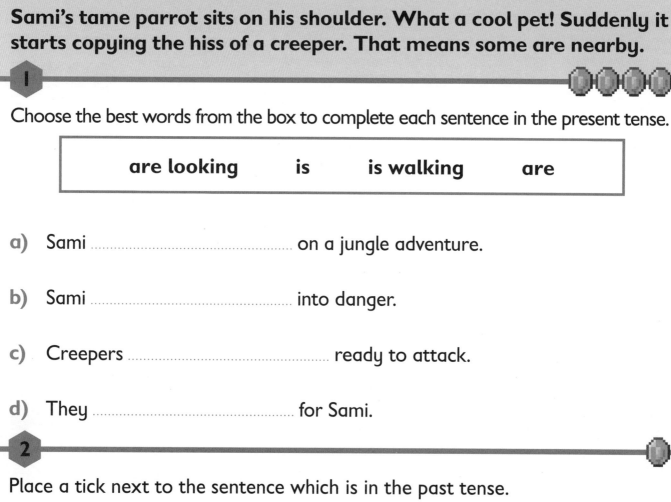

1

Choose the best words from the box to complete each sentence in the present tense.

are looking	is	is walking	are

a) Sami .... on a jungle adventure.

b) Sami .... into danger.

c) Creepers .... ready to attack.

d) They .... for Sami.

2

Place a tick next to the sentence which is in the past tense.

The creepers are near to him. ☐

The creepers were ready for him. ☐

Sami is aware of the creepers nearby. ☐

Through the trees, Sami can see the creepers. There are lots of them. Maybe it would be safer to sneak away than to fight them.

3

Rewrite the verb to show that there was an ongoing action in the past.

a) Sami walked quietly.

Sami was .... quietly.

b) The creepers hissed scarily.

The creepers were .... scarily.

c) Sami held his sword.

Sami was .... his sword.

d) Sami hoped he would be safe.

Sami was .... he would be safe.

4

Write a sentence in the present tense, saying what Sami is doing in this biome. Then write the same sentence in the past tense.

....

....

....

....

COLOUR IN HOW MANY EMERALDS YOU EARNED

PRESENT PERFECT FORM OF VERBS

The present perfect tense can be used instead of the past tense when referring to events that have happened before now (the present). The event is no longer happening. The present perfect form uses the present form of the verb *to have* and the past participle of the main verb.

Sami is very lucky. A rare ocelot is also sneaking through the jungle, and creepers stay away from these furry beasts!

In each sentence, underline the present form of *to have* and circle the main verb.

a) Sami has stayed close to the ocelot.

b) Creepers have kept their distance.

c) The trees have grown very tall.

d) A panda has spawned nearby.

Select the correct form of the main verb to complete each sentence in the present perfect tense.

a) The ocelot has .... the creepers. **scaring / scared**

b) The leaves have .... the bright sunlight. **blocked / blocking**

c) Sami has .... wood for shelter. **find / found**

d) His parrot has .... of danger. **warned / warn**

Sami and his parrot keep exploring. Sami climbs a tree and spies a jungle temple nearby. If only Kim was here to see it.

3

Complete each sentence using the correct present form of the verb *to have*.

a) They .... walked a long way.

b) Sami .... lit torches as trail markers.

c) A jungle temple .... generated nearby.

d) Melons .... been collected for food.

4

Write the given main verb in the correct form to ensure each sentence is in the present perfect tense.

a) Sami has .... Kim.   **miss**

b) A parrot has .... overhead.   **fly**

c) Sami and Kim have .... many adventures.   **have**

d) Four zombies have .... on the path ahead.   **appear**

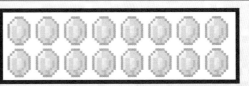
COLOUR IN HOW MANY EMERALDS YOU EARNED

FRONTED ADVERBIALS

An adverbial is a word or phrase used to add extra information to a verb. For example: *They went for a walk <u>on a beautiful, sandy beach</u>.* The adverbial phrase *on a beautiful, sandy beach* gives more detail about going for the walk. If the adverbial phrase appears at the beginning of a sentence, it is called a fronted adverbial. For example: *<u>On a beautiful, sandy beach,</u> they went for a walk.*

Sami just wants to get to the temple safely. Good luck, Sami!

Underline the adverbial phrase in each sentence.

a)   Sami walked through dense, humid jungle.

b)   His parrot warned him with a loud squawk.

c)   An ocelot was prowling, quietly and stealthily.

d)   Sami decided to rest after a short and easy fight.

Underline the fronted adverbial in each sentence.

a)   In the dark jungle, there were many dangers.

b)   During the night, it would be quite scary.

c)   When he saw more creepers, Sami decided to run.

d)   As the creepers approached, he saw the temple.

Sami has almost reached the temple. Not far now!

 3

Read the fronted adverbial and complete each sentence. Before you complete the sentences, ask yourself, 'What was on top of the hill or in the clearing?', or 'What happened on top of the hill or in the clearing?'

a)   On top of a hill, ...

....

b)   In a clearing, ...

....

4

Rewrite each sentence so that the adverbial phrase becomes a fronted adverbial.

a)   Sami searched for food after the battle.

....

b)   The creepers disappeared when they saw the ocelot.

....

c)   Sami spotted the jungle temple hidden behind the trees.

....

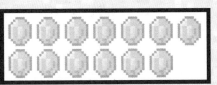
COLOUR IN HOW MANY EMERALDS YOU EARNED

THE POSSESSIVE APOSTROPHE

The possessive apostrophe is used to show that something belongs to somebody or something else (for example: *Sami's shelter*). The apostrophe in *Sami's* shows that the shelter belongs to him.

Sami runs into the temple, placing dirt blocks behind him to stop the mobs from following. He crafts a torch and begins to explore.

Draw lines to join each noun on the top row with the object that belongs to it in the bottom row.

the jungle's	Sami's	the torch's	his adventure's

end	sword	trees	glow

2

Add the possessive apostrophe to each of the words in bold in this passage.

It was **Samis** dream to find a jungle temple. He wished he had **Kims** help.

He found the level puzzle on the lower floor and looked at the **puzzles** levers.

He would have to pull them in the correct order to earn the **temples** treasures.

Sami looks at the three levers. Answer these questions to help.

3

Write a phrase, which uses a possessive apostrophe, about each of the following.

a)   a parrot belonging to Sami

....

....

b)   a diamond sword belonging to Kim

....

....

c)   a bow belonging to a skeleton

....

....

4

The highlighted nouns below are plural and end in s. Explain what you notice about the addition of the apostrophe.

| the panda **twins'** home | the **trees'** leaves |

....

....

 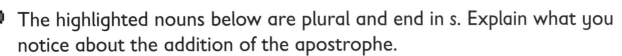

DIRECT SPEECH

Direct speech shows the exact words that a character says in your piece of writing. Direct speech is punctuated with inverted commas – they are placed around the exact words spoken. For example:
"*We must build a shelter,*" said Sami.

Sami will have to pull the levers until he finds the right combination.

 I

Underline the spoken words in each sentence below.

a)   Let me try this order, said Sami.

b)   Squawk, cried his parrot.

c)   Sami said, No that wasn't right.

 2

Add the missing inverted comma to show the direct speech in each of these sentences.

a)   I should try again," said Sami.

b)   "I wonder if this will work? asked Sami.

c)   Sami grumbled, This is too hard!"

Sami keeps trying different lever combinations. There is no way he is leaving the temple without getting the loot!

 3

Rewrite each of the sentences from question 1, using inverted commas to show the spoken words.

a) ....

b) ....

c) ....

4

Look at the two pieces of direct speech below. What other punctuation do you notice and where is it being used?

"I am not going to give up," said Sami.

"I got the order of the levers right," gasped Sami.

....

....

DETERMINERS A AND AN

Determiners come before a noun and give more information about that noun. The determiners *a* and *an* say what the noun is without being specific. For example: <u>*a*</u> *bird*, <u>*an*</u> *apple* – they don't refer to a particular bird or apple. The determiner *an* is used if the noun begins with a vowel (a, e, i, o or u), while *a* is used if the noun begins with a consonant (a letter that is not a vowel).

Sami has solved the temple's tricky lever puzzle! A chest is revealed. What treasures will he find inside?

 1

Choose the correct determiner, *a* or *an*, for each of the items Sami found in the chest.

a) .... diamond

b) .... enchanted book

c) .... iron ingot

d) .... bone

2

Write the correct determiner, *a* or *an*, into each space in the passage below.

Sami had found .... temple in .... jungle. He had tamed ....

parrot which warned him when .... angry mob was nearby. After solving the

lever puzzle in the temple, Sami earned .... chest full of cool loot.

As Sami walks around the corner, he sees a tripwire across the floor. Sami knows that if he breaks the wire then arrows will shoot out!

3

Choose the best noun from the box to add to each sentence. Use each one once.

pair of shears	tripwire	arrow	adventure

a) Sami spotted a ....

b) If Sami broke it, he might be hit by an ....

c) Sami managed to cut the wire with a ....

d) This was an .... of a kind he had never experienced before.

4

Explain what is wrong with the sentence below.

Sami found an chest with a emerald inside.

....

....

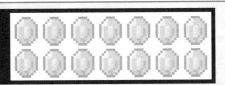

COMMAS

Commas can be used to separate items in a list. They are placed between each item in the list, apart from the final two items which are usually separated by *and* or *or*.

Sami leaves the temple, pleased with the items he has found. Above the trees he sees a firework. It must be a signal from Kim! He rushes to meet her and share their adventures so far.

1

Place a tick or cross under each comma to show whether it is used correctly or incorrectly.

a)   Kim liked the plains, jungle, mountain and cave biomes, the best.

☐ ☐   ☐

b)   Sami had fought, creepers, slimes, zombies and skeletons.

☐ ☐ ☐

2

Rewrite each sentence below, adding commas in the correct place.

a)   The jungle was a dark dangerous creepy and strange place.

....

b)   Creepers zombies witches and skeletons are some of the dangers.

....

c)   What adventures might lie ahead for Sami Kim and the parrot?

COLOUR IN HOW MANY EMERALDS YOU EARNED ◇◇◇◇◇◇◇◇◇◇◇

ADVENTURE ROUND-UP

FEATHERED FRIEND

Sami and Kim walk through the jungle together. Kim loves Sami's tame parrot. Sami admires Kim's new diamond sword.

RAVINE SEEN

Kim tells Sami that as she trekked through the trees by herself, she saw a huge, mysterious ravine. It has to be worth exploring! Sami agrees. Kim is excited. Another new adventure is about to begin!

COMPOSITION

DIGGING DOWN

Caves are a must for any Minecraft explorer. Digging underground to see what you can find is essential – and also awesome fun!

UNDERGROUND WONDERLAND

Whether you create your own tunnels and hollows, or stumble on a natural maze of caverns, the experience of the caves is always a thrill. Explorers should be careful not to let their guard down – caves are dark, and darkness means dangerous enemy mobs...

EXCITING POSSIBILITIES

Kim leads Sami to the edge of the jungle and shows him the ravine she had discovered. It is huge! A gigantic opening that leads deep inside the earth. They both know that it would be great fun to explore and might even contain some rare and valuable ore. They check their equipment and descend into the ravine...

EFFECTIVE WRITING

Writing can be made more effective by improving the descriptive words used (for example, by changing *big* to *huge* or *colossal*). Another way is to use pronouns (see page 30) to avoid repetition.

Deep in the ravine, Sami and Kim see a cave leading into the darkness.

1

Replace each of the underlined adjectives with the best word from the box that has a similar meaning.

evil	terrifying	vast	round

a) The cave looked <u>big</u> and dark.

b) From deep inside they heard a <u>scary</u> sound.

c) There could be an <u>awful</u> enemy mob in there.

2

Read the text below. Replace each of the underlined nouns with a suitable pronoun.

Kim prepared her diamond sword. The sword was heavy and <u>Kim</u> held the <u>sword</u> tight.

Sami took out his bow because he knew <u>Kim and Sami</u> might find danger in the cave.

NON-FICTION WRITING

Non-fiction writing can be a report, instructions, an explanation of something, a recount of events, or anything else that tells the reader factual (real) information.

It is now so dark in the cave that Sami has to craft torches and place them on the walls to see where they are going.

1

Tick the two factual sentences.

Kim found a cave.

Caves are lovely and made from cakes and sweets.

Sami uses torches to mark the way.

Parrots have four legs and long horns.

2

Write two sentences, each giving a fact about caves. Before you write, say your sentences aloud to check that they make sense.

....

....

Deeper and deeper, Sami and Kim continue into the cave. They think about the enemies that might be lurking below.

 3

Read each factual sentence and select the best word from the box to add to each of them.

Creepers	Zombies	Bats	Ghasts

a) .... are flying passive mobs that spawn in caves.

b) .... can approach silently before exploding.

c) .... are an undead mob that will burn in sunlight.

 4

Write a factual sentence about each of the given words. Do your sentences make sense? Read them aloud to make sure.

a) cave

....

b) skeleton

....

c) Enderman

....

COLOUR IN HOW MANY
EMERALDS YOU EARNED

ORGANISING NON-FICTION WRITING

Non-fiction texts are usually presented in a way to make it easier to find information within them. Headings are used to say what a page or a long section of text is about, and subheadings can be used to say what a shorter section or a paragraph is about. Facts can also be shown in tables and diagrams to make them easier to find and understand.

Sami's parrot has been suspiciously quiet. Maybe there are no mobs in this cave? That seems unlikely. They decide to stop and eat some food while thinking about the things they might encounter.

 1

Draw a line to join each heading on the left to the group of three subheadings on the right which fit best with it.

Hostile Mobs		Coal	Gold	Iron

Passive Mobs		Zombies	Creepers	Silverfish

Ores		Chickens	Ocelots	Bats

2

Write a sentence giving relevant information under each subheading.

a) Coal ....

....

b) Bats ....

....

As they chat about mobs by the light of their torches, Sami thinks about the mobs he has seen most on his adventures.

3

Organise the information in the text to present it in the table below.

During his adventures, Sami has seen over 150 mobs. He has seen 64 zombies mostly in forest biomes, 56 skeletons mostly in plains and mountain biomes, and 38 creepers in the plains biome.

Mob seen	Number of times

4

Write a paragraph of at least three sentences about torches. Check each sentence makes sense by saying it aloud before you write.

Torches

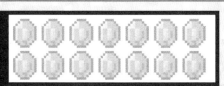

USING PARAGRAPHS

To help your writing make sense, organise it into paragraphs. Each paragraph should contain well-written sentences that share the same idea or topic. For example, one paragraph might describe a character or a setting, while another might explain an event in the story.

Sami and Kim continue deeper into the cave. A sinister moan makes them stop. A zombie comes shuffling out of the gloom.

Draw lines to join each sentence on the left with the paragraph it belongs to on the right.

Sentence	Paragraph
The zombie looked terrifying.	Describing how a character feels
Sami was looking forward to fighting the zombie.	Describing a setting
It was a darkness deeper than they'd ever seen.	Describing a character
Kim was usually alert to possible danger.	Describing a zombie

From the two choices given, circle the paragraph subheading that each sentence is most likely to be found under.

a) They will break after being used too much.   **Weapons / Villagers**

b) Zombies are one deadly example.   **Mountains / Hostile mobs**

c) They can hit mobs from a distance.   **Carrots / Arrows**

As Sami battles the zombie, Kim spots a spider sneaking up behind him. She jumps into action with her diamond sword!

3

Each sentence below should be organised into either paragraph 1 (describing the character) or paragraph 2 (describing an event). Write 1 or 2 at the end of each sentence to show which paragraph it is from.

a) The spider approached, looking more deadly as it got near.

b) Kim was a great fighter, always ready for action.

c) She swung her sword at the scuttling creature.

d) Kim carried a sword made from ore that she mined herself.

4

Write two paragraphs with three sentences in each. Say each sentence aloud before you write it. Describe one type of hostile mob in the first paragraph and describe another type in the second paragraph.

....

....

....

....

....

....

COLOUR IN HOW MANY EMERALDS YOU EARNED

WRITING ABOUT CHARACTERS

Characters in stories need to be interesting and believable. It can be a good idea to base them on somebody you know, as this will help you to describe how they look and behave. You should also describe how characters feel during the story.

After beating the enemy mobs, Sami and Kim come across a deep underground lake. They still haven't found any useful ore though.

1

Create a word bank to describe Kim or Sami. Think about how they look and how they move. Choose three adjectives and three adverbs.

Adjectives: ....

Adverbs: ....

2

Think about how Sami is feeling in the cave. Write a short paragraph of three sentences to describe how he is feeling and why.

....

....

....

....

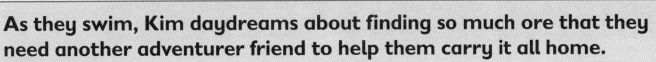

As they swim, Kim daydreams about finding so much ore that they need another adventurer friend to help them carry it all home.

3

Imagine that another character joins Sami and Kim on their mission. Then answer these questions about that character.

a) What is the character's name? ....

b) What do they look like (three adjectives)?

....

c) How do they move (three adverbs)?

....

d) How do they feel about going on an adventure?

....

4

Write a short paragraph describing the person you have started to think about in question 3.

....

....

....

....

 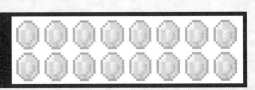

WRITING ABOUT SETTINGS

Giving a good description of a setting helps the reader to picture where a story takes place. It is often a good idea to base a setting on a place that you know, have seen or have read about. Say your sentences aloud to check that they make sense before you write them.

Sami and Kim emerge from the lake and find that they have swum into an enormous cavern. High on the walls they can see the glittering green glow of emerald ore. What a find!

1

Imagine the cavern that they have found. Write eight adjectives to describe it.

....

....

2

Write a short paragraph to describe the cavern. Use your ideas from question 1.

....

....

....

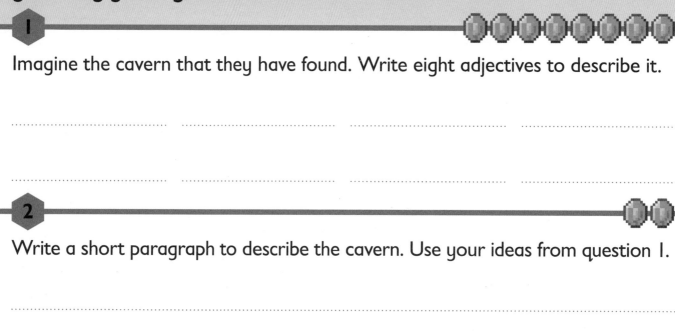

Sami and Kim get to work. Sami mines dirt blocks and places them so Kim can climb up and get the emerald ore.

3

Think about another place that Sami and Kim might have visited. Write three words in each column of the table to describe it.

What it looks like	What it smells like	Sounds that can be heard

4

Using your ideas from the table in question 3, write a short description of the setting you have thought about.

....

....

....

....

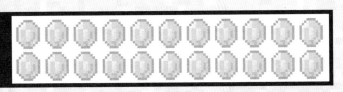

PROOFREADING

Proofreading helps to make sure that there are no mistakes in your spelling and punctuation. Correcting mistakes will make your writing easier to read and understand.

Kim and Sami are so busy mining the emerald ore that they don't notice Sami's parrot is hissing. Creepers are coming!

I

Underline the spelling and punctuation mistakes in the passage below. Rewrite the passage with these mistakes corrected.

Sami heard the hiss of the creepers to late. One exploded right next to him? Three more creepers were gliding across the cave towords them. Kim used her bow to shoot two of them before they could get too close. Sami tried, to fight the last one but his iron sword broke Thinking fast, Kim dropped her dymond sword from where she was standing and Sami quickly grabbed it. He defeeted the last creeper just in time?

....

....

....

....

....

....

COLOUR IN HOW MANY EMERALDS YOU EARNED

ADVENTURE ROUND-UP

SUFFERING SAMI

Sami and Kim find lots of precious emerald ore, but Sami is badly hurt in the fight with the creepers. Kim shares some of her food with him, and they sit and rest while his health is restored.

A BREAKTHROUGH

The large cavern they are in seems to be a dead-end with nowhere else to go.

"I suppose we should start digging," laughs Sami as they get to work with their pickaxes.

Suddenly they break through into an open space with wooden beams holding up the roof. They have found a mineshaft!

CREATIVE WRITING

CREEPY MINESHAFTS

If you spend enough time digging around underground, sooner or later you will find a mineshaft. These abandoned tunnels are a great place to find lots of useful ore, but they are also home to lots and lots of cave spiders!

MINECART TRACKS

If you are really lucky, you might even find an old, working redstone minecart track down there. All aboard!

READY OR-E NOT?

Sami and Kim break through from a maze of caverns into an old mineshaft. That means there must be ore waiting to be found, Get those pickaxes ready!

PLANNING 1

Planning your writing helps you to develop ideas and express them in a way that interests the reader. For non-fiction writing, you need to consider the different sections of text at the planning stage.

There are two tunnels leading away from Sami and Kim. They agree to split up and explore each one.

 1

Draw lines to join each description of a section of text to the subheading in the bottom row that it would best belong to.

Dangers in the mineshaft.	An explanation of what mineshafts are.	Writing about what mineshafts are like.

Mineshaft Features	**Mineshafts**	**Mineshaft Safety**

2

Write two ideas you might plan to write about under each subheading.

Hostile mobs ....

....

Survival ....

....

PLANNING 2

Stories should be well-planned and well-written. They need good description and an interesting plot (what happens in the story).

The pair set off separately to explore the tunnels and arrange to meet up again a short time later.

1

Think about the characters in this story, Sami and Kim.

a) What is Sami like?

....

....

b) What is Kim like?

....

....

2

Think about one of the places from this book as a story setting. Answer these questions about it.

a) What is this place like?

....

b) What dangers are there?

....

c) What might Sami and Kim find there?

....

Sami sets off down his tunnel. There are lots of cobwebs, and he has his sword ready in case of cave spider attacks.

3

Put these ideas for a story in the correct order by labelling them 1–4.

Sami and Kim are going on an adventure to find diamonds and ore to make weapons and armour. ☐

They find a mineshaft where they know there are diamonds. Their way is blocked by cave spiders and zombies. ☐

Sami manages to fight off cave spiders and zombies while Kim explores. He then helps and they find the diamonds. ☐

Sami and Kim are introduced as the main characters and the location they are in is described. ☐

4

♥ Plan a paragraph of writing to describe Sami fighting off cave spiders.

a) What weapon does he have? ....

b) What does he do first? ....

c) How does he feel? ....

d) What else does he do to fight the spiders? ....

e) How is he when the fight is over? ....

STORY WRITING 1

A story needs to keep the reader interested. A good opening will describe the characters and setting. It might also give a clue about what might happen in the story by explaining what the characters plan to do. To add excitement, a story often builds up to a problem that the characters face and must overcome.

Over in Kim's tunnel, she finds some blocks of iron ore and gets to work chipping them out with her pickaxe.

Plan the opening to a story. Your characters are Sami and Kim and they are in the mineshaft.

What is their mission?	How do they feel?	How have they prepared?

2

Using your ideas from question 1, write the part of the story opening that explains what the characters plan to do, how they feel and how they have prepared. Remember to say your sentences aloud before you write them.

....

....

....

....

Sami is attacked by cave spiders! Five of them come skittering out of the darkness, trying to bite him with their venomous fangs.

3

The characters in your story get close to where they need to be, but there is a problem. Think of key words and ideas to answer the following questions.

a) What is it like there?

....

b) What is the problem?

....

4

Write your ideas from question 3 as two short paragraphs for this part of your story. Make sure it is clear to the reader that your characters now face a problem. Read your sentences aloud to check that they make sense.

....

....

....

....

....

....

COLOUR IN HOW MANY EMERALDS YOU EARNED

STORY WRITING 2

Once a problem occurs in the plot of your story, you can describe how the characters deal with it. After that, you can move on to the story ending to explain if the characters achieved what they set out to do.

Kim is putting the last of the iron ore in her inventory when she hears the sound of Sami fighting echoing down the tunnels. She quickly draws her diamond sword and runs to help.

I

Think about the problem you thought of on page 65 for your story. Answer these questions to help you consider how the problem is resolved.

a)   Is there a danger and, if so, what is it?

....

b)   Do the characters need or use anything to help them?

....

c)   What key events take place in resolving the problem?

....

2

Using your notes from question I, describe how the problem in your story was resolved. Do your sentences make sense? Read them aloud to check that they do.

....

....

....

....

More cave spiders keep appearing but, working together, Sami and Kim manage to defeat them all. It is a long and scary battle!

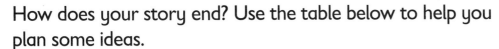

3

How does your story end? Use the table below to help you plan some ideas.

What happens?	Was the mission a success?	How do the characters feel?

4

Write your story ending using the notes you made in question 3. Remember to say your sentences aloud before you write them.

....

....

....

....

NON-FICTION WRITING 1

When writing non-fiction, each section should have a clear purpose. Subheadings can help and it is vital that facts are presented clearly. As with all writing, say your sentences aloud first and read them again after writing to make sure that they make sense.

Sami and Kim resume their exploring, but this time they stick together. As they go, they discuss the best ways to fight different mobs.

1

Kim and Sami want to write a book about mobs to help others if they come across them. The first section of the book will be an introduction to mobs. Answer the following questions to help you write an introduction for them.

a) What are mobs? ....

b) Where and when are they found? ....

....

c) What types of mobs are there? ....

....

2

Write a short introduction based on your answers in question 1.

....

....

....

....

....

Bats fly by as they walk the spooky mineshaft tunnels, mining any ore they find on the way – iron, copper, even some gold!

3

Imagine that Kim and Sami need to explain some of the different types of mobs in Minecraft. Write down key words in each section of the table below.

Passive mobs	Hostile mobs	Neutral mobs

4

Using the notes you made in question 3, write a short description of each type of mob under the subheadings below.

Passive mobs ....

....

Hostile mobs ....

....

Neutral mobs ....

....

NON-FICTION WRITING 2

In non-fiction writing, you can explore some ideas in great detail if you have a really good understanding of what you are writing about.

Sami almost trips over an old minecart track. This would be a fun ride, if they could find the cart. Kim spots two carts further down the track – surrounded by zombies!

1

Kim and Sami want to give the reader more information about zombies in their book about mobs. Write down notes for everything you know about zombies.

> **Zombies: notes**
>
>

2

Use the key information from your notes in question 1 to write a short paragraph about zombies. Remember to say your sentences aloud before you write them.

....

....

....

....

It's a good thing that Sami and Kim are as good at fighting as they are at mining. They battle the zombies to reach the old minecarts.

 3

The final part of Kim and Sami's book will be about how to defeat hostile mobs. Choose one mob that they could write about. Plan this section by answering the questions below.

a)   Which hostile mob have you chosen? ....

b)   What is the best way to defeat them? ....

c)   What weapons could be used? ....

 4

Use your answers in question 3 to write a paragraph about how to defeat your chosen mob.

....

....

....

....

EDITING

Editing your writing can help to improve it. Carefully read through what you write and think about how it sounds. This helps to identify where sentence structures could be improved and where the words used could be improved for better effect.

With the zombies defeated, Sami and Kim jump in the minecarts. There is a redstone switch nearby. Kim hits it and – whoosh! – off they go!

Read the text below. Rewrite it, changing the underlined words and the whole of the final sentence to make it sound more effective.

There are <u>loads of</u> ways to use redstone. It can power minecarts, which are a <u>good</u> way to travel. They can move <u>fast</u> on tracks and you ride them.

....

....

2

Choose two sentences from any of your writing in the earlier pages of this book. Write each sentence exactly as it was originally written, then write an edited and improved version beneath.

a)   Sentence 1: ....

   Sentence 1 edited: ....

b)   Sentence 2: ....

   Sentence 2 edited: ....

COLOUR IN HOW MANY EMERALDS YOU EARNED

ADVENTURE ROUND-UP

END OF THE RIDE

The minecarts come to a sudden halt at the end of the track. What an exciting way to finish their adventure!

ADVENTURE ACHIEVEMENTS

Kim and Sami make their way out of the mineshaft, back into the sunshine. They have new weapons, lots of useful and precious ore, and Sami got the pet parrot he always wanted! More importantly, they have lots of new stories from their adventure. Who knows what's next...

ANSWERS

Page 5

1 It seemed to just **dis**appear!
   Kim had **mis**placed her sword.
   Kim was **un**lucky to lose her diamond sword.

   [1 emerald each for underlining the prefix
   in the given words; 1 emerald each for joining the words to
   the correct sentences]

2 a) **un**usual   [1 emerald]
   b) **un**kind   [1 emerald]
   c) **mis**trust   [1 emerald]
   d) **un**tidy   [1 emerald]
   e) **dis**able   [1 emerald]
   f) **dis**obey   [1 emerald]

Pages 6–7

1 a) re   b) re   c) super
                              [1 emerald each]

2 a) autobiography   [1 emerald]
   b) interact   [1 emerald]
   c) submerged   [1 emerald]

3

Word	Prefix	Root word
reappear	re	appear
return	re	turn
interact	inter	act
refresh	re	fresh

                              [1 emerald each]

4 a) again or back   [1 emerald]
   b) against   [1 emerald]
   c) between   [1 emerald]
   d) self   [1 emerald]

Pages 8–9

1 start**ing**; expect**ed**; forgott**en**; frustr**ation**; grow**ing**
                              [1 emerald each]

2 a) begin   [1 emerald]
   b) prefer   [1 emerald]
   c) inform   [1 emerald]
   d) forget   [1 emerald]

3 a) relaxation   [1 emerald]
   b) confrontation   [1 emerald]
   c) temptation   [1 emerald]
   d) consideration   [1 emerald]

4 The answer should acknowledge that the lazy e at
   the end of the root word is dropped before adding
   the suffix -ation.   [1 emerald]

Pages 10–11

1 a) sadly   [1 emerald]
   b) completely   [1 emerald]
   c) finally   [1 emerald]
   d) actually   [1 emerald]
   e) honestly   [1 emerald]
   f) quickly   [1 emerald]
   g) exactly   [1 emerald]
   h) fairly   [1 emerald]

2 a) sensibly   [1 emerald]
   b) simply   [1 emerald]
   c) fiddly   [1 emerald]

3 feeble – feebly   [1 emerald]
   possible – possibly   [1 emerald]
   angry – angrily   [1 emerald]
   sad – sadly   [1 emerald]
   happy – happily   [1 emerald]
   complete – completely   [1 emerald]

4 If a word ends in -ic, add -ally instead of just -ly
                              [1 emerald]

Pages 12–13

1 a) dangerous   [1 emerald]
   b) venomous   [1 emerald]
   c) serious   [1 emerald]

2 enormous; curious; various; tremendous
                              [1 emerald each]

3 a) humorous   [1 emerald]
   b) glamorous   [1 emerald]
   c) rigorous   [1 emerald]

4 a) The y has been changed to an i before adding -ous.
                              [1 emerald]
   b) -ous is just added to the root word.   [1 emerald]
   c) The e is dropped before adding -ous.   [1 emerald]

Pages 14–15

1 late; plains; daisy; prey; eight   [1 emerald each]

2 double; trouble; touch; could   [1 emerald each]

3 Sentences will vary but must contain the given word
   used correctly.
   Examples:
   a) She had to wait until the time was right.
                              [1 emerald]
   b) She could feel the weight of her pickaxe in her hand.
                              [1 emerald]
   c) They knew she was there.   [1 emerald]
   d) She knew she would have to be brave. [1 emerald]

4 Example answers:

Long *a* using *ei*:   vein, rein, veil
Long *a* using *ey*:   prey, grey, they
Long *a* using *eigh*: weight, eight, sleigh
Short *u* using *ou*: double, could, would

[1 emerald each]

Pages 16–17

1 a) enough   [1 emerald]
  b) through   [1 emerald]
  c) Although   [1 emerald]
  d) thought   [1 emerald]
2 purpose – various – famous   [1 emerald each]
3 fear; hear; heart; heard; early; earth   [1 emerald each]
4 Sentences will vary but must contain the given word used correctly.
  Examples:
  a) She was so hungry and would love to have some fruit.   [1 emerald]
  b) Kim could write a guide about fighting zombies.   [1 emerald]
  c) It had been a busy adventure.   [1 emerald]

Pages 18–19

1 should not – shouldn't
  do not – don't
  she is – she's
  they have – they've
  you will – you'll
  you are – you're   [1 emerald each]
2 should not – shouldn't
  could have – could've
  she will – she'll
  was not – wasn't   [1 emerald each]
3 weren't; wouldn't; hadn't; she'd; I'll   [1 emerald each]
4 a) haven't – have not   [1 emerald]
  b) won't – will not   [1 emerald]
  c) she'd – she had or she would   [1 emerald]
  d) aren't – are not   [1 emerald]

Pages 20–21

1 creeper; whole; sword; village; zombie
                                      [1 emerald each]
2 a) chicken; cow; creeper   [1 emerald each]
  b) The explanation should acknowledge that the third letter (r) comes before the third letter of cow (w) in the alphabet.   [1 emerald]
3 Century is a **noun**.   [1 emerald]
  It means **one hundred years**.   [1 emerald]
4 a) busy – doing a lot or having a lot to do [1 emerald]
     business – activity or job   [1 emerald]
  b) 'business' comes before 'busy' as the fourth letter (i) comes before *y* in the alphabet.   [1 emerald]

Page 22

1 Rain; hear; plain; through; weather; not; there
                                      [1 emerald each]
2 eight – ate   meet – meat
  peace – piece   grate – great   [1 emerald each]

Page 25

1 a) although   [1 emerald]
  b) because   [1 emerald]
  c) but   [1 emerald]
2 Answers will vary. Ensure the conjunctions are used correctly.
  Examples:
  a) Sami could run away or hide.   [1 emerald]
  b) He knows he will get food if he searches everywhere.   [1 emerald]

Pages 26–27

1 a) because   [1 emerald]
  b) while   [1 emerald]
  c) when   [1 emerald]
2 a) because   [1 emerald]
  b) when   [1 emerald]
  c) as   [1 emerald]
3 while – time   as – cause
  when – time   because – cause   [1 emerald each]
4 a) because / as   [1 emerald]
  b) when / after   [1 emerald]
  c) as / when   [1 emerald]
  d) when / as / after   [1 emerald]

Pages 28–29

1 a) behind   [1 emerald]
  b) in   [1 emerald]
  c) on   [1 emerald]
  d) under   [1 emerald]
2 a) soon   [1 emerald]
  b) later   [1 emerald]
  c) outside   [1 emerald]
  d) nearby   [1 emerald]
3 Answers will vary. Each must be suitable.
  Examples:
  a) over   [1 emerald]
  b) onto   [1 emerald]
  c) before   [1 emerald]
  d) into   [1 emerald]
4 Sentences will vary but must contain the given word used correctly. **Examples:**
  a) He would catch the parrot soon.   [1 emerald]
  b) Sami could eat later.   [1 emerald]
  c) There were trees everywhere.   [1 emerald]
  d) His shelter was nearby.   [1 emerald]

Pages 30–31

1.
a) It   [1 emerald]
b) He   [1 emerald]
c) They   [1 emerald]
d) It   [1 emerald]

2.
a) It   [1 emerald]
b) He   [1 emerald]
c) They   [1 emerald]

3. he; it; they; it   [1 emerald each]

4.
a) his   [1 emerald]
b) theirs   [1 emerald]

Pages 32–33

1.
a) is   [1 emerald]
b) is walking   [1 emerald]
c) are   [1 emerald]
d) are looking   [1 emerald]

2. The creepers were ready for him.   [1 emerald]

3.
a) walking   [1 emerald]
b) hissing   [1 emerald]
c) holding   [1 emerald]
d) hoping   [1 emerald]

4. Answers will vary but each must be in the correct tense.
Examples:
Present: Sami is hiding from the creepers.
Past: Sami was hiding from the creepers.
      [1 emerald each]

Pages 34–35

1.
a) has (stayed)   [1 emerald]
b) have (kept)   [1 emerald]
c) have (grown)   [1 emerald]
d) has (spawned)   [1 emerald]

2.
a) scared   [1 emerald]
b) blocked   [1 emerald]
c) found   [1 emerald]
d) warned   [1 emerald]

3.
a) have   [1 emerald]
b) has   [1 emerald]
c) has   [1 emerald]
d) have   [1 emerald]

4.
a) missed   [1 emerald]
b) flown   [1 emerald]
c) had   [1 emerald]
d) appeared   [1 emerald]

Pages 36–37

1.
a) through dense, humid jungle   [1 emerald]
b) with a loud squawk   [1 emerald]
c) quietly and stealthily   [1 emerald]
d) after a short and easy fight   [1 emerald]

2.
a) In the dark jungle   [1 emerald]
b) During the night   [1 emerald]
c) When he saw more creepers   [1 emerald]
d) As the creepers approached   [1 emerald]

3. Answers will vary. **Examples:**
a) there were several zombies.   [1 emerald]
b) he fought the creepers.   [1 emerald]

4.
a) After the battle, Sami searched for food. [1 emerald]
b) When they saw the ocelot, the creepers disappeared.   [1 emerald]
c) Hidden behind the trees, Sami spotted the jungle temple.   [1 emerald]

Pages 38–39

1. the jungle's trees   Sami's sword
the torch's glow   his adventure's end
      [1 emerald each]

2. Sami's; Kim's; puzzle's; temple's   [1 emerald each]

3.
a) Sami's parrot   [1 emerald]
b) Kim's diamond sword   [1 emerald]
c) a skeleton's bow   [1 emerald]

4. The answer should acknowledge that the apostrophe in each is placed after the s.   [1 emerald]

Pages 40–41

1.
a) Let me try this order   [1 emerald]
b) Squawk   [1 emerald]
c) No that wasn't right   [1 emerald]

2.
a) "I should try again."   [1 emerald]
b) "I wonder if this will work?"   [1 emerald]
c) "This is too hard!"   [1 emerald]

3.
a) "Let me try this order," said Sami.   [1 emerald]
b) "Squawk," cried his parrot.   [1 emerald]
c) Sami said, "No that wasn't right."   [1 emerald]

4. The answer should acknowledge that a comma is used before the end of the direct speech, helping to separate the direct speech from the person who said it.
      [1 emerald]

Pages 42–43

1. a) a   b) an   c) an   d) a   [1 emerald each]

2. a temple; a jungle; a parrot; an angry mob; a chest
      [1 emerald each]

3.
a) tripwire   [1 emerald]
b) arrow   [1 emerald]
c) pair of shears   [1 emerald]
d) adventure   [1 emerald]

4. The explanation should acknowledge that an should be replaced by a before the word 'chest' and that a should be replaced by an before the word 'emerald'.
      [1 emerald]

Page 44

1 a) plains, [✓]   jungle, [✓]   biomes, [✗]
                                    [1 emerald each]
   b) fought, [✗]   creepers, [✓]   slimes, [✓]
                                    [1 emerald each]
2 a) The jungle was a dark, dangerous, creepy and
       strange place.   [1 emerald for each comma]
   b) Creepers, zombies, witches and skeletons are
       some of the dangers.   [1 emerald for each comma]
   c) What adventures might lie ahead for Sami, Kim
       and the parrot?   [1 emerald for the comma]

Page 47

1 a) vast   [1 emerald]
   b) terrifying   [1 emerald]
   c) evil   [1 emerald]
2 Kim – she
   sword – it
   Kim and Sami – they   [1 emerald each]

Pages 48–49

1 Kim found a cave. [✓]
   Sami uses torches to mark the way. [✓]
                                    [1 emerald each]
2 Answers will vary but must be factual and make sense.
   Examples:
   Caves are dark places. Some caves are very large.
                        [1 emerald each for each sentence]
3 a) Bats   [1 emerald]
   b) Creepers   [1 emerald]
   c) Zombies   [1 emerald]
4 a)–c) Each sentence should be correctly constructed
          and initially said aloud. Each should relate to
          the given subject. [1 emerald for each sentence]

Pages 50–51

1 Hostile Mobs – Zombies, Creepers, Silverfish
                                    [1 emerald]
   Passive Mobs – Chickens, Ocelots, Bats   [1 emerald]
   Ores – Coal, Gold, Iron   [1 emerald]
2 a)–b) Each sentence should be correctly constructed
          and be about the given subject.   [1 emerald each]
3

Mob seen	Number of times
Zombies	64
Skeletons	56
Creepers	38

                                    [1 emerald each]
4 Each sentence in the paragraph should be correctly
   constructed and initially said aloud. Each should relate to
   the subject of torches.   [1 emerald for each sentence
                                    up to a maximum of 3]

Pages 52–53

1 The zombie looked terrifying.
     – Describing a zombie
   Sami was looking forward to fighting the zombie.
     – Describing how a character feels
   It was a darkness deeper than they'd ever seen.
     – Describing a setting
   Kim was usually alert to possible danger.
     – Describing a character   [1 emerald each]
2 a) Weapons   [1 emerald]
   b) Hostile mobs   [1 emerald]
   c) Arrows   [1 emerald]
3 a) 2   b) 1
   c) 2   d) 1   [1 emerald each]
4 Each paragraph should contain at least three
   correctly constructed sentences, with each
   paragraph about a different hostile mob.
                        [1 emerald for each sentence
                        up to a maximum of 6]

Pages 54–55

1 Answers will vary. **Examples:**
   Adjectives: tall; happy; strong
   Adverbs: quickly; carefully; smartly   [1 emerald each]
2 The paragraph should contain three correctly
   constructed sentences and describe how Sami feels in
   the cave and why (or more).
                        [1 emerald for each sentence]
3 a)–d) Answers will vary.   [1 emerald each]
4 The paragraph should contain three (or more)
   correctly constructed sentences and describe the
   character.   [1 emerald for each sentence up to a
                                    maximum of 3]

Pages 56–57

1 Answers will vary.
   Examples:
   huge; vast; cold; dark; green; damp; smelly; spooky
                                    [1 emerald each]
2 The paragraph should contain at least two correctly
   constructed sentences and describe the cave. Each
   sentence must have at least one adjective from
   question 1.   [1 emerald for each sentence up to
                                    a maximum of 2]
3 Answers will vary but the words must describe the
   setting being considered.   [1 emerald for each word]
4 The paragraph should contain three (or more)
   correctly constructed sentences and describe the
   setting from question 3. Each sentence must have at
   least one adjective from question 3.
                        [1 emerald for each sentence
                        up to a maximum of 3]

Page 58

1 Sami heard the hiss of the creepers <u>to</u> (too) late. One exploded right next to him<u>?</u> (.) Three more creepers were gliding across the cave <u>towords</u> (towards) them. Kim used her bow to shoot two of them before they could get too close. Sami tried<u>,</u> (comma not needed) to fight the last one but his iron sword broke_ (.) Thinking fast, Kim dropped her <u>dymond</u> (diamond) sword from where she was standing and Sami quickly grabbed it. He <u>defeeted</u> (defeated) the last creeper just in time<u>?</u> (.)

[1 emerald for each corrected mistake]

Page 61

1 Dangers in the mineshaft. – Mineshaft Safety
An explanation of what mineshafts are.
– Mineshafts
Writing about what mineshafts are like.
– Mineshaft Features   [1 emerald each]

2 Answers will vary.
Examples:
Hostile mobs: different mobs; why each is dangerous
[1 emerald]
Survival: building shelters; finding food   [1 emerald]

Pages 62–63

1 a) Answers will vary. Check that they are suitable for Sami.   [1 emerald]
b) Answers will vary. Check that they are suitable for Kim.   [1 emerald]

2 a)–c) Answers will vary depending on the chosen setting.   [1 emerald each]

3 Sami and Kim are introduced as the main characters and the location they are in is described.   1
Sami and Kim are going on an adventure to find diamonds and ore to make weapons and armour.   2
They find a mineshaft where they know there are diamonds. Their way is blocked by cave spiders and zombies.   3
Sami manages to fight off cave spiders and zombies while Kim explores. He then helps and they find the diamonds.   4
[1 emerald each]

4 a)–e) Answers will vary. Full sentences not required.   [1 emerald each]

Pages 64–65

1 Answers will vary.   [1 emerald for each column]

2 Each sentence in the paragraph should be correctly constructed and initially said aloud. The content should include what the characters plan to do, how they feel and how they prepared.
[1 emerald for each of these ideas]

3 a)–b) Answers will vary. Each part should contain at least two key words or ideas.
[1 emerald for each part]

4 Each paragraph should contain at least two correctly constructed sentences. The content should also make it clear that the characters face a problem.
[1 emerald for each paragraph;
1 emerald for mentioning the problem faced]

Pages 66–67

1 a)–c) Answers will vary.   [1 emerald each]
2 Answers will vary. Ensure the response includes: what the characters do and/or use; at least one key event in solving the problem; coherent sentences.
[1 emerald for each of these]
3 Answers will vary.   [1 emerald for each column]
4 Answers will vary. Ensure the sentences are correctly constructed, and the three main ideas of what happens, whether the mission was a success and feelings are included.   [1 emerald for each idea]

Pages 68–69

1 Answers will vary. **Examples:**
a) Mobs are beings or creatures.   [1 emerald]
b) Mobs are found in every biome and the more dangerous ones are usually found in the dark.
[1 emerald]
c) There are hostile mobs, passive mobs, neutral mobs and boss mobs.   [1 emerald]

2 Answers will vary but must contain the information from above.
[1 emerald for each piece of information used]

3 Answers will vary. Words used can also give examples of each type of mob.
Passive mobs: never attack; not dangerous; most are breedable; most can be tamed.
Hostile mobs: will attack; dangerous; aggressive
Neutral mobs: only attack if provoked or attacked
[1 emerald for ideas in each column]

4 Answers will vary. Sentences should be correctly constructed and contain at least one piece of information about the type of mob.   [1 emerald each]

Pages 70–71

1 Answers will vary. Information could include:
Hostile mob; undead mob; do not like light; burn in sunlight; make groaning sounds   [1 emerald for each piece of information up to a maximum of 3]

2 Answers will vary. Sentences should be correctly constructed and contain three (or more) ideas/pieces of information about zombies.
[1 emerald for each idea up to a maximum of 3]

3 a)–c) Answers will vary.   [1 emerald each]

4   Answers will vary. Sentences should be correctly
     constructed and contain three (or more) ideas/pieces
     of information based on the responses to question 3.
          [1 emerald for each idea up to a maximum of 3]

Page 72

1   Answers will vary.
     Examples:
     loads of: many; numerous; several   **[1 emerald]**
     good: great; fun; exciting   **[1 emerald]**
     You can ride them and they can move quickly/
     speedily down the tracks.   **[1 emerald]**

2   **a)–b)** Answers will vary. Discuss what has been
             changed and why.   **[1 emerald each]**

TRADE IN YOUR EMERALDS!

That was quite an adventure! Remember the jungle temple filled with traps? And the creepy mineshaft full of zombies? Kim and Sami couldn't have done it without your help. Thank you!

Now it's your turn. Imagine you are going on your own Minecraft adventure. Add up all the emeralds you earned throughout this book, and decide what to buy from the trader to help you on your way.

Write the total number of emeralds you earned in this box:

HMMM?

SHOP INVENTORY

- DIAMOND CHESTPLATE: 30 EMERALDS
- DIAMOND HELMET: 20 EMERALDS
- DIAMOND BOOTS: 20 EMERALDS
- DIAMOND SWORD: 25 EMERALDS
- NETHERITE PICKAXE: 30 EMERALDS
- NETHERITE SWORD: 35 EMERALDS
- ARROWS OF POISON: 15 EMERALDS
- ARROWS OF HEALING: 15 EMERALDS
- ENCHANTED BOOK: 15 EMERALDS
- GOLDEN APPLE: 10 EMERALDS
- GOLDEN CARROT: 15 EMERALDS
- COOKED PORKCHOP: 5 EMERALDS
- POTION OF REGENERATION: 30 EMERALDS
- POTION OF LEVITATION: 25 EMERALDS
- POTION OF INVISIBILITY: 35 EMERALDS

That's a lot of emeralds. Well done! Remember, just like real money, you don't need to spend it all. Sometimes it's good to save up.